IT'S A FACT!

Real-Life Reads

Disgusting ANIMAL Defenses

by Ruth Owen

Consultant:

Suzy Gazlay, MA
Recipient, Presidential Award for Excellence in Science Teaching

Ruby Tuesday Books

Published in 2014 by Ruby Tuesday Books Ltd.

Editor: Mark J. Sachner
Designer: Emma Randall
Production: John Lingham

Photo Credits:
FLPA: Cover, 4, 11, 13, 18–19; J. J. Harrison: 23; Nature Picture Library:
8–9; NOAA Okeanos Explorer Program: 10; Tim Ransom: 28–29;
Shutterstock: 5, 6–7, 14–15, 17 (bottom), 21, 22, 26–27, 29 (bottom), 31;
Superstock: 12, 16–17, 20, 24–25.

Library of Congress Control Number: 2013920132

ISBN 978-1-909673-64-9

Printed and published in the United States of America

For further information including rights and permissions requests, please
contact our Customer Service Department at 877-337-8577.

CONTENTS

It's Going to Get Disgusting!

Life for many animals is a daily struggle to avoid being eaten. So it's no surprise that some creatures have developed extreme ways to stay safe from their enemies.

Fulmar chick

This fluffy fulmar chick looks cute. Get too close, though, and you'll be wearing the baby bird's lunch!

Sea cucumber

Then there's the sea cucumber. How much damage can a slow-moving creature with no brain actually do? We've got just two words to say to you. Spaghetti attack.

Hoopoe bird

And don't be fooled by the hoopoe bird's good looks. This creature looks much better than it smells.

So get ready to see some disgusting animal defenses in action. You're going to be horrified. You're going to be grossed out. But most of all, you will be truly amazed!

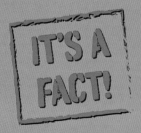
IT'S A FACT!

5

Horned Lizards

Horned lizards are **reptiles** that live in hot, dry deserts in North America.

These lizards feed on ants, grasshoppers, beetles, and spiders. They search for their **prey** in wide-open places. As they hunt, horned lizards are in danger from **predators** such as birds, snakes, coyotes, and dogs.

Horned lizard

A camouflaged horned lizard

If a predator comes close, a horned lizard uses **camouflage** to hide. It flattens its body onto the stony, sandy ground and blends in. Camouflage doesn't always work, however.

A Bloody Defense

Sometimes, coyotes and dogs use their sense of smell to sniff out a camouflaged lizard. If this happens, a horned lizard has a final, bizarre way to defend itself.

When under attack, a horned lizard shoots jets of blood from its eyes. The blood can squirt six feet (1.8 m) into the air. The lizard's predator gets splattered with blood. As the surprised attacker figures out what to do next, the lizard runs away!

DON'T MESS WITH ME!

Horrifying Hagfish

In cold oceans around the world lives a creature called the hagfish.

Hagfish

Mouth

Hagfish may look like snakes or eels, but they are neither. Hagfish are also not actually fish. In fact, scientists are still trying to figure out what animal family these creatures belong to.

Hagfish are **scavengers** that eat the dead bodies of other animals. They search for **carcasses** on the seabed. Once a hagfish finds a carcass, it burrows into the dead body. Then it feeds on the rotting flesh.

Hagfish

Slime Attack!

Hagfish share their ocean home with many predators. But if an enemy tries to bite a hagfish, the attacker soon regrets its choice of meal.

Hagfish

Slime

A scientist's hand covered with hagfish slime

When under attack, a hagfish releases huge amounts of slime from its body. The attacker's mouth is instantly filled with thick, disgusting goo. Choking on a mouthful of slime, the predator usually decides to leave the hagfish alone.

Even fearsome hunters such as sharks don't go back for a second bite of hagfish!

SLIMED!

Sea Cucumbers

The sea cucumber's name makes it sound like a strange vegetable. It may even look like one. But it's actually an ocean animal.

Sea cucumbers are **invertebrates**. This means they have no backbone or skeleton. There are hundreds of different types of sea cucumber. Some types are just one inch (2.5 cm) long. Others are longer than an adult human.

These slow-moving creatures spend their lives on the seabed. Any predator that thinks a sea cucumber is an easy meal, however, soon gets a horrible, sticky surprise!

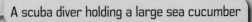
A scuba diver holding a large sea cucumber

Sea cucumber

A Cucumber Fights Back

When under attack from a predator, a sea cucumber shoots a mass of sticky threads out of its backside.

Suddenly, the attacker becomes the attacked. The spaghetti-like strings wrap around the predator's body. The animal may even be harmed by poisons in the strings. The predator struggles to break free of the clinging, poisonous threads. As it does, the sea cucumber slowly makes its escape.

Crab

CUCUMBER ATTACK!

A black sea cucumber

Threads

A leopard sea cucumber

Sticky threads

Beautiful Hoopoes

Sometimes, very beautiful creatures defend themselves in very disgusting ways.

Hoopoes are colorful birds that live in parts of Europe, Africa, and Asia. Hoopoes raise their chicks inside holes in trees.

Many different predators eat hoopoe chicks if they get the chance. So, to keep predators away from its nest, a hoopoe family makes quite a stink!

Female hoopoe

Nest hole

Chick

Home Sweet Home

Once a female hoopoe has chicks, her body produces a foul-smelling liquid. The liquid comes from a **gland** near her tail. Using her beak, the hoopoe rubs the liquid through her feathers.

The hoopoe chicks also produce the same smelly liquid and rub it on their feathers. Pretty soon, the whole family smells like rotting meat. The disgusting smell keeps most predators away from the nest.

If a predator dares to enter the nest, the chicks defend themselves in another way. They blast their attacker with jets of stinking poop!

A hoopoe chick in its nest

PRETTY
STINKY!

Fulmars

Fulmars are large seabirds that live in many parts of the world. They spend most of their lives out at sea, catching fish.

In spring, fulmars come to shore to mate and raise chicks. Each pair of birds chooses a ledge on a steep cliffside to be their nest. Then the female bird lays a single egg.

Nests high on a steep cliff are safe from most predators. But fulmars and their chicks are often attacked by other seabirds.

A fulmar sitting on its nest

Fulmar

Vomit Attack!

If a predatory bird gets too close to a fulmar's nest, it soon realizes it has made a big mistake.

To defend its egg or chick, a fulmar blasts its enemy with a jet of oily, fishy vomit. The fulmar can hit a target 10 feet (3 m) away.

It's not just adult fulmars that vomit on their enemies. Sometimes a predator tries to mess with a fulmar chick. Then the baby bird unleashes its own defensive vomit attack!

BACK OFF, BIRD EATER!

Vomit

Fulmar chick

Leaf Beetle Larvae

Birds, insects, and other predators make life for a fat, juicy beetle **larva** very dangerous. The larvae of leaf beetles have a truly disgusting way to stay safe, however.

There are thousands of different types of leaf beetles. Female leaf beetles lay their eggs on leaves. A larva hatches from each egg and starts greedily feeding on leaves. To avoid becoming another animal's meal, the larva builds itself a protective shield.

What does it make the shield from? We're very glad you asked.

Cereal leaf beetle

Leaf beetle eggs

A Colorado potato beetle larva

Protective Poop Shields

A leaf beetle larva builds its protective shield from its own poop.

Walking around covered with poop may sound disgusting. It's a very good way, however, to keep from being eaten.

Cereal leaf beetle larva

Leaf beetles make their poop shields in many different designs. Some types of leaf beetle larvae even have poisonous poop shields. These poisons don't hurt the larvae, but they do harm predators that eat the poisonous poop.

IT'S GROSS, BUT IT'S A FACT!

Shield made of poop

Red lily beetle larva

Poop

Glossary

camouflage (KAM-uh-flahzh)
The way that an animal blends in with its background to hide from predators or its prey. For example, an animal's skin color or pattern may be its camouflage.

carcass (KAR-kuhss)
A dead body. This word is usually used to describe the dead body of an animal.

gland (GLAND)
An organ in a person's or animal's body that produces chemical substances.

invertebrate (in-VUR-tuh-brit)
An animal without a backbone. Insects, worms, snails, sea cucumbers, and starfish are all invertebrates.

larva (LAR-vuh)
A young insect that looks like a fat worm. Many insects have four life stages, which are egg, larva, pupa, and adult.

predator (PRED-uh-tur)
An animal that hunts and eats other animals.

prey (PRAY)
An animal that is hunted by other animals for food.

reptile (REP-tile)
A cold-blooded animal with scaly skin. Lizards, snakes, turtles, crocodiles, and alligators are all reptiles.

scavenger (SCAV-in-jer)
An animal that usually eats the carcasses of dead animals. Some types of scavengers eat poop or dead plants.

Index

Read More

Owen, Ruth. *Creepy Backyard Invaders (Up Close and Gross: Microscopic Creatures).* New York: Bearport Publishing (2011).

Wood, Alix. *Amazing Animal Camouflage (WOW! Wildlife).* New York: Rosen Publishing (2013).

Learn More Online

To learn more about disgusting animal defenses, go to
www.rubytuesdaybooks.com/disgustingdefenses